Mug Cake Recipes

That Actually Work!

Vicky Wells

Copyright© 2016 by Vicky Wells

Library of Congress Control Number: 2016917390

All rights reserved

No part of this book may be used or reproduced in any manner whatsoever without prior written permission from the publisher, except for the inclusion of brief quotations in reviews.

Cover Artwork & Design by
Old Geezer Designs

Published in the United States by
Victoria House Bakery Secrets
an imprint of
DataIsland Software LLC,
Hollywood, Florida

ebooks.geezerguides.com

ISBN-10: 0-692-03286-X

ISBN-13: 978-0-692-03286-2

Neither the author nor the publisher assumes responsibility for errors in internet addresses or for changes in the addresses after publication. Nor are they responsible for the content of websites they do not own.

Table of Contents

Why Make Cake in a Mug? 1
- History of Mug Cakes 1
- Why Do These Recipes Actually Work? 1
- Test with Your Own Microwave 2
- Use only Fresh, Quality Ingredients 2
- Citrus Juice and Zest 3
- Size and Type of Mug 3
- Greasing the Mug 4

Getting It Right 5
- Don't Overcook 5
- Don't panic! 5
- Why Take the Cake Out of the Mug? 6

Basic Vanilla Mug Cake 7

Basic Chocolate Mug Cake 8

Apple Crisp in a Mug 9

Apple Raisin Mug Cake 10

Bailey's Mug Cake 11

Banana Mug Cake with Cream Cheese Frosting 12

Berry Cobbler in a Mug 14

Blueberry Mug Cake 15

Boozy Rum Raisin Mug Cake 16

Carrot Cake in a Mug 17

Crustless Cheesecake in a Mug 18

Chocolate Butterscotch Chip Mug Cake 19
Chocolate Chip Cookie Dough Mug Cake 20
Chocolate Coconut Mug Cake 21
Chocolate Peanut Butter Mug Cake.. 22
Chocolate Espresso Mug Cake 23
Cinnamon Honey Raisin Mug Cake 24
Cinnamon Roll in a Mug................ 25
Coffee Cake in a Mug................ 26
Cranberry Mug Cake 27
Egg Nog Mug Cake 28
Gingerbread Mug Cake 29
Lemon Mug Cake................ 30
Maple Walnut Mug Cake 31
Mocha Mug Cake................ 32
Nutella Mug Cake................ 33
Peach Cobbler in a Mug................ 34
Peanut Butter Cookie in a Mug............ 35
Peanut Butter, Honey and Banana Mug Cake 36
Sour Cream Cake in a Mug 37

STICKY BUTTERSCOTCH MUG CAKE............ 38
PUMPKIN PIE SPICE APPLESAUCE
MUG CAKE 39
PUT DE LIME IN DE COCONUT MUG CAKE .. 40
RED VELVET CAKE IN A MUG 41
STRAWBERRY CHEESECAKE IN A MUG......... 42
SUGAR COOKIE IN A MUG 43
SWEET POTATO MUG CAKE 44
WALNUT ESPRESSO MUG CAKE.................... 45
HOMEMADE PUMPKIN PIE SPICE 46
   Bonus Recipe 46
WIN A MUG 47
ABOUT OUR COOKBOOKS 48
   Quality 48
   Consistency.. 48
   Only Quality Ingredients 48
ABOUT THE AUTHOR..................................... 49

Why Make Cake in a Mug?

Mug cakes are a quick and easy way to make an individual serving.

With lots of creative and interesting recipes, you don't need to make a traditional cake to enjoy a tasty dessert or snack.

There's minimal clean up, too.

History of Mug Cakes

Most of us have tried mug cakes, at least once, since they first burst on the culinary scene.

I've tried to research when the first mug cake was actually invented/introduced but with little success.

If memory serves, I remember making my first mug cake at least 20 years ago. I guess they showed up a little while after microwave ovens became mainstream. According to Wikipedia, the first counter top microwave oven, produced by Amana Corporation, was introduced in 1967. They appear to have become ubiquitous in the 1990s.

Why Do These Recipes Actually Work?

While doing lots of research and testing for this cookbook, I discovered that using full power for most mug cake recipes resulted in a less-than-perfect outcome. Many of the cakes appeared to be done but, when they were turned out of the mug, up to one-third of the dough was uncooked.

Adding additional time at full power resulted it an tough, dry dough that made for an unpleasant eating experience.

After a lot of testing, and some spectacular failures, I discovered that the best approach was a lower power for a longer time.

You'll find that most of the recipes in this cookbook are microwaved at half-power (50%) for four to four-and-a-half minutes.

I believe that the resulting cake is more evenly cooked, has a better texture and turns out of the mug more easily.

Test with Your Own Microwave

Microwaves vary, so the times and power levels given in this cookbook may not work exactly in your microwave.

Here's the microwave I used - An Electrolux 1000 Watt Microwave. This is considered average. However, microwaves can range anywhere from 400 to 1100 watts.

Check the wattage on your microwave so you can more easily determine the power setting that will work best for you.

As I have used Power Level 5 (half-power) for most of these recipes, I'm making the assumption that that relates to about 500 watts of power. So, if your microwave is only 500 watts, then you would need to use full power, if it's 700 watts, then you would likely use Power Level 8 … you get the idea.

Use only Fresh, Quality Ingredients

While developing the recipes for this book I came across a lot of mug cake recipes that use cake mixes, pudding mixes, jello mixes, artificial sweeteners, egg substitutes and more.

You will never find any low quality or artificial ingredients in any of my cookbooks.

It takes little to no additional effort to use fresh, quality ingredients.

And besides, we're worth it and deserve only the best!

Imperial and Metric

Each recipe in this cookbook has both Imperial and Metric measurements so that all of our readers will be able to make these mug cakes without having to worry about looking up conversions.

What Kind of Oil Should I Use?

Many of the recipes call for olive oil or coconut oil. The main reason I use these oils is for quality (lower quality oils can affect the taste and cooking results) and batter consistency (olive oil will give you a thinner batter while coconut oil will produce a thicker batter). Often I'll use coconut oil when I want a thicker batter for the mug cake. For instance, I used coconut oil in the Maple Walnut Mug Cake so that the thicker batter would prevent the walnuts from sinking to the bottom of the mug while it cooked.

Citrus Juice and Zest

From time-to-time, recipes call for freshly squeezed lemon, lime or orange juice and/or freshly grated lemon, lime or orange zest.

For smaller recipes, such as these, it can seem like a waste to squeeze and zest such a little bit. What happens to the rest?

Whenever a recipe needs either of these, I like to to zest the entire fruit first (it's easier to zest an intact fruit than one that's already been juiced). Then I juice it.

Any zest or juice that is left over can easily be frozen.

Zest, in particular, freezes very well and can be used frozen in any recipe that calls for it.

Juice, of course, would need to be thawed before using.

If you do this, you'll always have some "freshly squeezed" and "freshly zested" citrus available for your recipes!

Size and Type of Mug

I have tested these recipes in either a 15 oz. microwave-safe ceramic mug, or a 16 oz microwave-safe glass measuring cup.

It's best if the mug you use is a little over-sized rather than under-sized.

Having said that, though, it is also a good practice to place the mug on a micro-wave safe plate, just in case you get an overflow.

After all, it's much easier to clean a plate than to clean your microwave. Am I right?

Greasing the Mug

In each of these recipes you'll be starting with a greased mug.

Do what works best for you. You can use coconut oil, olive oil, butter, etc. or a non-stick cooking spray.

For most of the recipes in this book, I have used a non-stick cooking spray and it has worked quite well.

Getting It Right

Getting your mug cake just right is as much of an art as it is a science. All microwaves are slightly different and have different power capabilities. The more mug cakes you make, the better you'll get at working with your microwave to create the perfect outcome.

How to Tell When Your Mug Cake is Done

In most of these recipes you'll find instructions to microwave on Power Level 5 (half-power) for approximately 4 minutes or until done. But, how do you tell if it's done?

The easiest way to check is, to insert a toothpick into the cake. If the toothpick comes out clean, it's done. If it doesn't, then keep microwaving, 10 seconds at a time, until it's done.

Hint: Sometimes I've thought it was done, the toothpick came out clean. However, when I turned it out, a lot of the batter near the bottom wasn't cooked. That's what lead me to develop the method of using a lower power for a longer time. But, as mentioned above, you will need to experiment with your own microwave to get the time/power level balance just right.

Don't Overcook

Now that you know how to check for doneness, you also need to be sure not to overcook your mug cake.

An overcooked mug cake can become tough and rubbery. Not the experience we're looking for at all.

Don't panic!

While your mug cake is cooking, it will look like it's precariously close to overflowing the mug.

Don't panic. As long as you have selected a mug that is large enough, that won't happen.

It will, however, during the cooking process, sometimes rise above the lip of the mug. But, it will settle back down.

Tip: Always place the mug on a microwave-safe plate or saucer, just in case there is an overflow.

Let It Cool

I know it's tempting to just dig right in when your cake comes out of the microwave. It just smells so good!

But, let it cool or you might burn your mouth.

It will cool even faster if you turn it out of the mug. Run a flat knife around the inside of the mug and slide it out onto a plate to cool. It should slide out easily if you've greased the mug. If you forgot to do that, it might take a little more "persuasion."

Why Take the Cake Out of the Mug?

I like to take the cake out of the mug before eating it for three reasons:

1. To be absolutely certain it is fully cooked

2. It cools faster that way

3. It's easy to share (Frequently, when I'm testing and developing these recipes, my husband and I will share the results. He loves it when I'm developing new recipes and he gets to be the "guinea pig".)

Basic Vanilla Mug Cake

This basic vanilla cake is quick and easy and can be dressed up however you like - ice cream, custard, fresh fruit, chocolate and/or caramel syrup. It's your choice.

It's also good just by itself.

Ingredients

>   4 Tbsp (30 g) all-purpose flour
>   ½ tsp (2.5 mL) baking powder
>   3 Tbsp (35 g) sugar
>   ½ Tbsp (7.5 mL) butter, softened
>   4 Tbsp (60 mL) milk
>   ½ tsp (2.5 mL) vanilla
>   Pinch of salt

Method

In a greased mug, combine all the ingredients for the cake and mix well to form a smooth batter.

Microwave on Power Level 5 (half-power) for 4 to 4½ minutes, or until done.

Basic Chocolate Mug Cake

I know there are people in this world that actually don't like chocolate cake, but I can't imagine there's very many of them.

When you need a quick, tasty chocolate fix, give this a try.

Ingredients

¼ cup (30 g) all-purpose flour
¼ cup (25 g) white sugar
2 Tbsp (30 mL) unsweetened cocoa powder
⅛ tsp (0.5 mL) baking soda
⅛ tsp (0.5 mL) salt
3 Tbsp (45 mL) milk
1 Tbsp (30 mL) vegetable oil
1 Tbsp (15 mL) water
¼ tsp (1.5 mL) vanilla

Method

In a greased mug, combine all the ingredients for the cake and mix well to form a smooth batter.

Microwave on Power Level 5 (half-power) for 4 to 4½ minutes, or until done.

Apple Crisp in a Mug

A favorite fall treat, but sometimes you just want a "taste". So, if you don't want to bake an entire apple crisp, whip together this smaller version and enjoy!

Ingredients

    1 apple, cored, peeled and thinly sliced
    1 Tbsp (14 g) quick oats*
    1 Tbsp (14 g) all-purpose flour
    ⅛ tsp (0.5 mL) ground cinnamon
    1 Tbsp (14 g) brown sugar, packed
    1 Tbsp (15 mL) butter

Method

Place the sliced in a greased mug and cover with plastic wrap. Microwave on high for one minute.

Mix remaining ingredients in a separate bowl until well combined and spoon over the apples.

Microwave on Power Level 5 (half-power) for 3 minutes.

It will be very hot so let it cool for approximately 5-10 minutes.

*If you don't have quick oats, you can put some old fashioned oats in a food processor and pulse it for a few seconds. Quick oats are just regular oats cut smaller so they cook faster.

Apple Raisin Mug Cake

This is a very moist cake and may need, depending on your microwave, the full 4½ minutes on half-power.

Ingredients

>1 egg
>3 Tbsp (45 mL) unsweetened applesauce
>2 Tbsp (30 mL) coconut oil, softened
>⅛ tsp (0.5 mL) vanilla
>⅛ tsp (0.5 mL) baking powder
>¼ tsp (1 mL) cinnamon
>3 Tbsp (35 g) brown sugar, packed
>5 Tbsp (38 g) all-purpose flour
>1 Tbsp (14 g) (20 g) raisins

Method

Combine all ingredients (except the raisins) in a greased mug and mix well.

Fold in the raisins to distribute evenly throughout the dough.

Microwave on Power Level 5 (half-power) for 4 to 4 1/2 minutes, or until done.

Hint: You may want to use one of the "snack" size applesauce cups if you don't want to open a whole jar of applesauce. There's enough in one of these ½ cup servings to make two of these mug cakes and have a little left over to use as a topping.

Bailey's Mug Cake

This lovely, spongy cake can be used for special occasions - like Tuesdays! Just kidding - sort of.

Ingredients

    1 egg
    3 Tbsp (45 mL) Bailey's (or similar liqueur)
    3 Tbsp (45 mL) olive oil
    6 Tbsp (45 g) all-purpose flour
    ⅛ tsp (0.5 mL) baking powder
    4 Tbsp (30 g) sugar

Garnish

    1 Tbsp (15 mL) Bailey's (or similar liqueur)
    1 Tbsp (15 mL) heavy cream

Method

Combine all ingredients in a greased mug and mix until smooth.

Microwave on Power Level 5 (half-power) for 4 - 4 1/2 minutes, or until done.

To garnish, mix the tablespoon of Bailey's and the tablespoon of heavy cream and pour over the cake.

Banana Mug Cake with Cream Cheese Frosting

This cake takes a little more time, and a few more ingredients, than a standard mug cake. But it's moist, tasty and practically irresistible. This one is even big enough for two (but we won't make you share).

Ingredients

Cake

    1/3 cup (40 g) all-purpose flour
    ¼ cup (25 g) sugar
    ¼ tsp (1.5 mL) baking powder
    ⅛ tsp (0.5 mL) salt
    ⅛ tsp (0.5 mL) ground cinnamon
    1 tsp (5 mL) olive oil
    ½ banana, very ripe, mashed
    1 egg
    1 Tbsp (15 mL) cream (or milk)
    ¼ tsp (1.5 mL) vanilla extract
    1 Tbsp (14 g) chopped walnuts or pecans

Frosting

    1 Tbsp (30 mL) cream cheese, softened
    2 tsp (10 mL) maple syrup

Method

In a small bowl, combine the ingredients for the frosting. Mix until smooth and creamy. Set aside.

In a greased mug, combine all of the dry ingredients. Mix well.

In a separate bowl or measuring cup, combine the liquid ingredients, including the mashed banana and mix well.

Add the liquid ingredients to the dry ingredients and mix well

Microwave on Power Level 5 (half-power) for 4 1/2 to 5 minutes, or until done.

Allow cake to cool for 5-10 minutes and then frost with the cream cheese mixture.

Note: This cake takes a little longer than most. In my 1000 watt microwave it took 4 minutes and 50 seconds.

Warning: Be sure to use a 15/16 oz. mug for this recipe, it needs it.

Tip: As this recipe calls for half a banana, why not serve it banana slices (from the left over half) on the side?

Berry Cobbler in a Mug

This cobbler, featuring real fruit, is so good that it makes enough to share! Get out another mug so you can share with someone else. Or, keep them both for you. I won't tell anyone. I promise!

Ingredients

    3/4 cup berries, fresh or frozen (works well with strawberries, raspberries or blueberries or any combination of these)
    4 Tbsp (30 g) powdered sugar
    1/3 cup (40 g) all-purpose flour
    1 Tbsp (14 g) granulated sugar
    1 Tbsp (15 mL) butter
    ½ tsp (2.5 mL) baking powder
    1 Tbsp (30 mL) whole milk or cream

Method

Evenly distribute the berries between two greased mugs (note: if using strawberries, make sure they are sliced). Sprinkle 1 Tbsp (14 g) of powdered sugar in each mug and mix to coat.

In a small bowl or measuring cup, combine the dry ingredients and mix well.

Add the butter to the flour mixture and mix well.

Add the milk (or cream) to the flour mixture and stir to create a smooth batter.

Spoon equal amounts of the batter into each mug.

Microwave each mug separately, on Power Level 5 (half-power), for 4 to 4½ minutes, or until done.

Once they have cooled, top with whipped cream or ice cream, if desired

Blueberry Mug Cake

This recipe is reminiscent of a blueberry muffin (my favorite kind).

Ingredients

1 egg
1 Tbsp (30 mL) coconut oil (softened)
⅛ tsp (0.5 mL) vanilla
⅛ tsp (0.5 mL) baking powder
¼ cup (50 g) sugar
¼ cup (30 g) all-purpose flour
2 Tbsp (20 g) blueberries, fresh or frozen

Method

Mix all ingredients (except the blueberries) in a greased mug until well combined.

Place the blueberries in the ¼ cup measure and dust with a little flour, tossing the blueberries to coat them with the flour (this should stop them from sinking to the bottom of the mug). Then, gently fold in the blueberries so they are evenly spread throughout the dough.

Microwave on Power Level 5 (half-power) for 4 to 4½ minutes, or until done.

Boozy Rum Raisin Mug Cake

You'll need to plan ahead for this recipe as the raisins need to be soaked in rum for at least two hours.

Ingredients

> 2 Tbsp (20 g) raisins
> 1 Tbsp (30 mL) rum
> 1 egg
> 1 Tbsp (15 mL) butter (at room temperature)
> ½ tsp (2.5 mL) rum extract
> 3 Tbsp (35 g) sugar
> 5 Tbsp (38 g) all-purpose flour
> ⅛ tsp (0.5 mL) baking powder

Method

In a small dish, combine the 1 Tbsp (30 mL) raisins and 1 Tbsp (30 mL) rum and allow the raisins to soak in the rum for at least 2 hours (overnight would be better).

In a greased mug, combine all of the ingredients (except the rum and raisin mixture), and mix well to form a smooth batter (it will be really thick).

Add the raisins, including any of the rum that has not been absorbed and mix again to distribute the raisins throughout the batter.

Microwave on Power Level 5 (half-power) for 4 to 4-½ minutes, or unit done.

Carrot Cake in a Mug

This cake is lovely and moist (as a carrot cake should be) and works equally well with or without the walnuts and raisins.

Ingredients

Cake

- 1 egg
- ½ small carrot, grated
- 1 Tbsp (15 mL) coconut oil, softened
- ⅛ tsp (0.5 mL) vanilla
- ⅛ tsp (0.5 mL) baking powder
- ¼ tsp (1.5 mL) cinnamon
- 3 Tbsp (35 g) brown sugar, packed
- ¼ cup (30 g) all-purpose flour
- ½ Tbsp (10 g) walnuts, chopped (optional)
- ½ Tbsp (10 g) raisins (optional)

Frosting

(After all, what's carrot cake without the cream cheese frosting?)

- 1 Tbsp (30 mL) cream cheese, softened
- 2 tsp (10 mL) maple syrup

Method

Mix all ingredients (except the walnuts and raisins) in a greased mug until well combined.

Gently fold in the walnuts and raisins so they are evenly spread throughout the dough.

Microwave on Power Level 5 (half power), or until done.

While the cake is cooking, cream together the cream cheese and maple syrup.

Allow the cake to cool for a minute or two and then top with the cream cheese frosting.

Crustless Cheesecake in a Mug

You'll need to be a bit patient with this recipe. It must cool completely. As a matter of fact, it's even better if your refrigerate for an hour or so before eating.

Ingredients

    3 Tbsp (35 g) sugar
    2 oz (56 g) cream cheese, softened
    ¼ tsp (1.5 mL) vanilla
    1 Tbsp (30 mL) sour cream
    1⅓ tsp (8 mL) lemon juice, freshly squeezed
    1 egg

Method

In a greased mug, combine all ingredients and mix until well-blended.

Microwave on high for 30 seconds, stir and microwave for an additional 30 seconds.

If it is not quite done, stir again and microwave in increments of 10 seconds.

Allow cheesecake to cool completely and then refrigerate for up to an hour (If you can wait that long - I couldn't!)

Top with fresh fruit and whipped cream, if desired.

Chocolate Butterscotch Chip Mug Cake

Chocolate and butterscotch! Does it get any better than this?

Ingredients

- 1 egg
- 3 Tbsp (45 mL) milk
- 3 Tbsp (45 mL) oil
- ⅛ tsp (0.5 mL) vanilla
- ¼ tsp (1.5 mL) cinnamon
- 4 Tbsp (30 g) light brown sugar
- 4 Tbsp (30 g) all-purpose flour
- ⅛ tsp (0.5 mL) baking powder
- 2 Tbsp (20 g) butterscotch baking chips
- 2 Tbsp (20 g) semi-sweet chocolate chips

Method

In a greased mug, combine all of the ingredients (except for the butterscotch and chocolate chips) and mix well to make a smooth batter.

Fold in the butterscotch and chocolate chips so that they are evenly dispersed in the batter.

Microwave on Power Level 5 (half-power) for 4 to 4½ minutes, or until done.

Chocolate Chip Cookie Dough Mug Cake

Tastes like chocolate chip cookie dough, but it's cooked!

Ingredients

    1 egg
    1 Tbsp (15 mL) butter, softened
    ¼ tsp (1.5 mL) vanilla
    ⅛ tsp (0.5 mL) baking powder
    1/3 cup (40 g) all-purpose flour
    3 Tbsp (35 g) light brown sugar, packed
    3-4 Tbsp (30 g) mini chocolate chips

Method

In a greased mug, beat egg and mix in the liquid ingredients.

Add the dry ingredients (except for the chocolate chips) and mix well, removing all lumps.

Fold in the chocolate chips so that they are evenly dispersed in the batter.

Microwave on Power Level 5 (half-power) for 4 to 4½ minutes or until done.

Chocolate Coconut Mug Cake

The addition of sour cream to this recipe makes it moist and gives it a little "tang", too.

Ingredients

1 egg
1 Tbsp (30 mL) sour cream
1 Tbsp (15 mL) oil
⅛ tsp (0.5 mL) vanilla
4 Tbsp (30 g) sugar
2 Tbsp (30 mL) unsweetened cocoa powder
4 Tbsp (30 g) all-purpose flour
⅛ tsp (0.5 mL) baking powder
2 Tbsp (20 g) shredded coconut

Method

In a greased mug, beat egg and mix in the liquid ingredients.

Add the dry ingredients (except for the coconut) and mix well, removing all lumps.

Fold in the coconut so that it is evenly dispersed in the batter.

Microwave on Power Level 5 (half-power) for 4 to 4½ minutes, or until done.

Chocolate Peanut Butter Mug Cake

Chocolate! And peanut butter! Together! In a cake! All I can say is - YES!

Ingredients

    1 egg
    1 Tbsp (15 mL) chunky natural peanut butter
    1 Tbsp (30 mL) milk
    1 Tbsp (30 mL) coconut oil
    ⅛ tsp (0.5 mL) vanilla
    ⅛ tsp (0.5 mL) (0.5 mL) baking powder
    4 Tbsp (30 g) sugar
    2 Tbsp (30 mL) unsweetened cocoa powder
    4 Tbsp (30 g) all-purpose flour

Method

In a greased mug, combine all of the ingredients and mix well to make a smooth batter.

Microwave on Power Level 5 (half-power) for 4 to 4½ minutes, or until done.

Chocolate Espresso Mug Cake

Get ready for that caffeine hit! This cake delivers on it big time with both chocolate and espresso. It also delivers on big time flavor, too.

Ingredients

    1 egg
    1 Tbsp (30 mL) veg. oil
    ½ tsp (2.5 mL) vanilla
    1 Tbsp (30 mL) milk
    3 Tbsp (25 g) all-purpose flour
    1 tsp (5 mL) instant espresso granules
    2 Tbsp (30 g) cocoa powder
    3 Tbsp (35 g) sugar
    ¼ tsp (1.5 mL) baking powder

Method

In a greased mug, combine all of the ingredients and mix well to make a smooth batter.

Microwave on Power Level 5 (half-power) for 4 to 4½ minutes, or until done.

Dust with powdered sugar, if desired.

Cinnamon Honey Raisin Mug Cake

This recipe makes a nicely textured and tasty cake. If you have trouble with the raisins sinking to the bottom, dust them with a little flour before incorporating them into the batter.

Ingredients

    1 egg
    3 Tbsp (45 mL) honey
    1 Tbsp (30 mL) oil (maybe substitute unsweetened apple sauce)
    ⅛ tsp (0.5 mL) vanilla
    4 Tbsp (30 g) all-purpose flour
    ⅛ tsp (0.5 mL) baking powder
    ¼ tsp (1.5 mL) cinnamon
    2 Tbsp (40 g) raisins

Method

In a greased mug, combine all of the ingredients (except the raisins) and mix well to make a smooth batter.

Fold in the raisins so that they are evenly dispersed in the batter.

Microwave on Power Level 5 (half-power) for 4 to 4½ minutes, or until done.

Cinnamon Roll in a Mug

An alternative to buying a calorie-dense, gooey cinnamon roll. Get all of the taste with a smaller, make-it-yourself serving.

Ingredients

¼ cup all-purpose flour
1 Tbsp (30 mL) whole milk or 10% cream
¼ tsp (1.5 mL) baking powder
1 Tbsp (15 mL) maple syrup
¼ tsp (1.5 mL) vanilla extract
1 tsp (5 mL) coconut oil
¼ tsp (1.5 mL) ground cinnamon
1 Tbsp (14 g) brown sugar, packed

Method

In a greased mug, add the first six ingredients. Mix well to form a thick batter.

Separately, mix together the brown sugar and cinnamon and sprinkle over the batter.

Use a knife, or bamboo skewer to create a swirl pattern on the top of batter.

Microwave on Power Level 5 (half-power) for 4 to 4½ minutes, or until done.

Coffee Cake in a Mug

You can put together this individual serving size coffee cake while the coffee is brewing.

Ingredients

Cake

    1 Tbsp (15 mL) butter, melted
    2 Tbsp (23 g) brown sugar
    1 Tbsp (30 mL) Greek yogurt
    ⅛ tsp (0.5 mL) vanilla extract
    ⅛ tsp (0.5 mL) baking powder
    ¼ tsp (1.5 mL) ground cinnamon
    ⅛ tsp (0.5 mL) ground nutmeg
    ⅛ tsp (0.5 mL) salt
    ¼ cup (30 g) all-purpose flour

Topping

    1 Tbsp (15 mL) cold butter
    2 Tbsp (15 g) all-purpose flour
    1 Tbsp (14 g) brown sugar
    ¼ tsp (1.5 mL) ground cinnamon

Method

In a greased mug, mix all of the ingredients for the "cake" part together, making sure everything is well mixed.

In a separate dish, mix together all of the ingredients for the "topping", using a fork. Crumble the topping mixture on top of the cake mixture.

Microwave on Power Level 5 (half-power) for 4 to 4½ minutes, or until done.

Cranberry Mug Cake

Next time you have a big turkey dinner with all the trimmings, save some of the cranberry sauce so you can make this yummy cranberry cake.

Ingredients

    1 egg
    1 Tbsp (30 mL) Greek yogurt (or sour cream)
    1 Tbsp (30 mL) whole berry cranberry sauce
    ⅛ tsp (0.5 mL) vanilla
    ⅛ tsp (0.5 mL) baking powder
    ¼ tsp (1.5 mL) cinnamon
    4 Tbsp (30 g) sugar
    4 Tbsp (30 g) all-purpose flour

Method

In a greased mug, beat egg and mix in the liquid ingredients including the cranberry sauce.

Add the dry ingredients and mix well to make a smooth batter.

Microwave on Power Level 5 (half-power) for 4 to 4½ minutes, or until done.

Egg Nog Mug Cake

A quick, festive treat!

You may want to save this one as a special treat at Christmas time when egg nog and candy canes are more readily available.

Ingredients

    4 Tbsp (30 g) all-purpose flour
    4 Tbsp (30 g) sugar
    1 egg
    3 Tbsp (45 mL) egg nog
    3 Tbsp (45 mL) olive oil
    Whipped cream (for garnish)
    Ground nutmeg (for garnish)
    Crushed candy cane (for garnish)

Method

In a greased mug, combine the flour and sugar. Mix well.

Add the egg and mix well.

Add the egg nog and the olive oil. Mix until smooth.

Microwave on Power Level 5 (half-power) for 4 to 4½ minutes, or until done.

Garnish with whipped cream, nutmeg and/or crushed candy cane.

Gingerbread Mug Cake

Gingerbread is one of my favorites and this recipe lets you indulge without making a whole cake.

Ingredients

>1 egg
>1 Tbsp (30 mL) molasses
>1 Tbsp (30 mL) olive oil
>⅛ tsp (0.5 mL) vanilla
>⅛ tsp (0.5 mL) baking powder
>¼ tsp (1.5 mL) ground ginger
>4 Tbsp (30 g) light brown sugar (packed)
>4 Tbsp (30 g) all-purpose flour

Method

In a greased mug, beat egg and mix in the liquid ingredients.

Add the dry ingredients and mix well, to form a smooth batter.

Microwave on Power Level 5 (half-power) for 4 to 4½ minutes, or until done.

Dust with powdered sugar, if desired.

Lemon Mug Cake

A truly lemon-y, lemon cake. Gotta love the flavor boost from freshly squeezed lemon and lemon zest!

Ingredients

Cake:

    1½ Tbsp (23 mL) lemon juice, freshly squeezed
    3 Tbsp (25 g) all-purpose flour
    1 Tbsp (30 mL) olive oil
    ⅛ tsp (0.5 mL) salt
    ¼ tsp (1.5 mL) baking powder
    1 tsp (5 mL) lemon zest, freshly grated
    3 Tbsp (35 g) sugar
    1 large egg

Frosting:

    1½ Tbsp (23 mL) lemon juice, freshly squeezed
    1/3 cup (35 g) icing sugar

Method

In a greased mug, combine all the ingredients for the cake and mix well to form a smooth batter.

Microwave on Power Level 5 (half-power) for 4 to 4½ minutes, or until done.

In a separate dish, mix the lemon juice with the icing sugar until it become smooth and then pour over the cake.

Maple Walnut Mug Cake

Be sure to use REAL maple syrup in this recipe to get the authentic taste.

Ingredients

    1 egg
    4 Tbsp (60 mL) maple syrup (the real stuff - NOT pancake syrup)
    1 Tbsp (30 mL) coconut oil
    ⅛ tsp (0.5 mL) vanilla
    ⅛ tsp (0.5 mL) maple extract (optional but boosts the maple flavor)
    ⅛ tsp (0.5 mL) baking powder
    4 Tbsp (30 g) all-purpose flour
    1 Tbsp (28 g) chopped walnuts

Method

In a greased mug, beat egg and mix in the liquid ingredients.

Add the dry ingredients (except walnuts) and mix well, removing all lumps.

Fold in the walnuts so that they are evenly dispersed in the batter.

Microwave on Power Level 5 (half-power) for 4 minutes or until done.

Let the cake cool for a few minutes before eating.

Mocha Mug Cake

Chocolate and coffee together - the perfect marriage!

Ingredients

1 egg
1 Tbsp (30 mL) olive oil
1 Tbsp (15 mL) half & half (can substitute regular whole milk or almond milk)
⅛ tsp (0.5 mL) vanilla
⅛ tsp (0.5 mL) baking powder
¼ tsp (1.5 mL) instant coffee granules (or use instant espresso granules for an extra "kick")
4 Tbsp (30 g) granulated white sugar
1 Tbsp (28 g) unsweetened cocoa power
4 Tbsp (30 g) all-purpose flour

Method

In a greased mug, beat egg and mix in the liquid ingredients.

Add the dry ingredients and mix well, removing all lumps.

Microwave on Power Level 5 (half-power) for 4 to 4½ minutes, or until done.

Nutella Mug Cake

Decadent, moist and delicious are the best words to describe this cake for one. (after all, who's going to share?)

Ingredients

> 1 egg
> 1 Tbsp (15 mL) unsweetened applesauce
> 1½ Tbsp (23 mL) coconut oil
> 1½ Tbsp (23 mL) Nutella (or similar chocolate/hazelnut spread)
> 3 Tbsp (45 mL) milk
> 3 Tbsp (25 g) all-purpose flour
> 1 Tbsp (14 g) cocoa powder
> ¼ tsp (1.5 mL) baking powder
> 1 Tbsp (14 g) sugar

Method

Combine all ingredients in a greased mug and mix well to form a smooth batter.

Microwave at Power Level 5 (half-power) for 4 to 4½ minutes, or until done.

Top with whipped cream or ice cream (whatever flavor you prefer), if desired.

Peach Cobbler in a Mug

Any easy way to make a quick, fruity dessert.

Ingredients

 1 egg
 1 Tbsp (15 mL) olive oil
 ⅛ tsp (0.5 mL) vanilla
 ⅛ tsp (0.5 mL) baking powder
 ¼ tsp (1.5 mL) ground cinnamon
 4 Tbsp (30 g) light brown sugar (packed)
 4 Tbsp (30 g) all-purpose flour
 1 Tbsp (28 g) chopped peaches (fresh or canned)

Method

In a greased mug, beat egg and mix in the liquid ingredients.

Add the dry ingredients (except peaches) and mix well, removing all lumps.

Fold in the peaches so that they are evenly dispersed in the batter.

Microwave on Power Level 5 (half-power) for 4 to 4½ minutes, or until done.

Peanut Butter Cookie in a Mug

This batter is a little thicker than most and is cooked for a shorter period of time to get a more "cookie" than cake effect. Actually, it's almost a cookie dough - but, because it's cooked you have no worries about raw egg. It will be a little moister and stickier than a mug cake.

Ingredients

    1 egg
    3 Tbsp (45 mL) peanut butter (smooth or chunky)
    1 Tbsp (30 mL) coconut oil
    1 Tbsp (28 g) sugar
    ¼ tsp (1.5 mL) vanilla extract
    ⅛ tsp (0.5 mL) baking powder
    4 Tbsp (30 g) all-purpose flour

Method

In a greased mug, combine all ingredients. Mix well to form a smooth batter.

Microwave on Power Level 5 (half-power) for 3 to 3½ minutes, or until done.

Peanut Butter, Honey and Banana Mug Cake

This classic combination of flavors produces a moist and tasty cake for all those peanut butter and banana sandwich lovers out there.

Ingredients

    1 egg
    ½ ripe banana, mashed
    1 Tbsp (30 mL) peanut butter (smooth or chunky)
    1 Tbsp (30 mL) honey
    ⅛ tsp (0.5 mL) vanilla
    ⅛ tsp (0.5 mL) baking powder
    ¼ tsp (1.5 mL) ground cinnamon
    4 Tbsp (30 g) all-purpose flour

Method

In a greased mug, beat egg and mix in the wet ingredients, including the mashed banana.

Add the dry ingredients and mix well, removing all lumps.

Microwave on Power Level 5 (half-power) for 4 to 4½ minutes, or until done.

Sour Cream Cake in a Mug

This is a moist cake thanks to the addition of sour cream. It's lovely topped with chocolate or butterscotch sauce, if you like.

Ingredients

    1 egg
    1 Tbsp (30 mL) sour cream
    1 Tbsp (15 mL) butter (at room temperature)
    ⅛ tsp (0.5 mL) vanilla
    ⅛ tsp (0.5 mL) baking powder
    3 Tbsp (35 g) light brown sugar (packed)
    4 Tbsp (30 g) all-purpose flour
    ¼ tsp (1.5 mL) lemon or orange zest

Method

In a greased mug, combine all ingredients and mix well, until a smooth batter is achieved.

Microwave on Power Level 5 (half-power) for 4 to 4½ minutes, or until done.

Sticky Butterscotch Mug Cake

This sticky butterscotch cake is more like a British-style pudding cake and amazingly tasty.

Substitute 10% cream for the milk for a richer, smoother flavor.

Ingredients

¼ cup (30 g) all-purpose flour
¼ cup (45 g) brown sugar, packed
½ tsp (2.5 mL) baking powder
1 Tbsp (15 mL) butter, softened
Pinch salt
3 Tbsp (45 mL) milk
½ tsp (2.5 mL) butterscotch extract (you can substitute vanilla extract if you don't have butterscotch)

Method

Mix all ingredients in a greased mug until well combined.

Microwave on Power Level 5 (half-power) for 4 minutes, or until done.

Pumpkin Pie Spice Applesauce Mug Cake

An great Fall recipe, when everything seems to be about pumpkin. But, did you know that pumpkin pie spice and apple go really well together? Get your Pumpkin Pie Spice fix without having to open a whole can of pureed pumpkin.

Ingredients

1 egg
3 Tbsp (45 mL) unsweetened applesauce
⅛ tsp (0.5 mL) vanilla
⅛ tsp (0.5 mL) baking powder
1 tsp (5 mL) pumpkin pie spice*
4 Tbsp (30 g) light brown sugar (packed)
5 Tbsp (38 g) all-purpose flour

Method

In a greased mug, combine all of the ingredients and mix well to create a smooth batter.

Microwave on Power Level 5 (half-power) for 4 to 4-½ minutes, or until done.

Top with any leftover applesauce and sprinkle with some Pumpkin Pie Spice mixed with sugar, if you like.

*See Bonus Recipe for how to make your own Pumpkin Pie Spice.

Put de Lime in de Coconut Mug Cake

A little bit of the tropics in your mug!

Ingredients

    1 egg
    4 Tbsp (60 mL) canned coconut milk (full fat)
    ½ tsp (2.5 mL) lime juice
    3 Tbsp (35 g) sugar
    4 Tbsp (30 g) flour
    ¼ tsp (1.5 mL) lime zest
    1 tsp (5 mL) coconut flakes

Method

In a greased mug, combine the first 4 ingredients and mix well, removing all lumps.

Fold in the lime zest and coconut flakes.

Microwave on Power Level 5 (half-power) for 4 to 4½ minutes, or until done.

Red Velvet Cake in a Mug

Red velvet cake is an absolute classic! Did you know that the original recipe used beets to supply the red coloring? If you don't want to use red food coloring, you could always replace it with beet juice.

Ingredients
Cake
- 1 egg
- 3 Tbsp (45 mL) buttermilk (or cream)
- 3 Tbsp (45 mL) olive oil
- 4 Tbsp (50 g) sugar
- ½ tsp (2.5 mL) red food coloring
- 4 Tbsp (30 g) all-purpose flour
- 1½ Tbsp (23 mL) unsweetened cocoa powder
- ⅛ tsp (0.5 mL) baking powder

Frosting
- ½ cup powdered sugar
- 1 Tbsp (30 mL) cream cheese, softened
- 1 Tbsp (30 mL) butter, softened

Method

In a greased mug, combine all the ingredients for the cake. Mix well to form a smooth batter.

Microwave on Power Level 5 (half-power) for 4 to 4½ minutes, or until done.

In a small mixing bowl, combine all the ingredients for the frosting. Whip by hand or use and electric mixer, until light and fluffy.

Spread frosting on the cake.

Strawberry Cheesecake in a Mug

The taste of the mug cake is simply divine. Even though it doesn't have a graham cracker crust, mixing in graham cracker crumbs completes the flavor of this timeless dessert.

Ingredients

- 1 egg
- 1 Tbsp (15 mL) cream cheese, softened
- 1 Tbsp (15 mL) ricotta cheese
- 1 Tbsp (30 mL) olive oil
- 1 Tbsp (15 mL) strawberry jam (homemade or store-bought)
- ⅛ tsp (0.5 mL) vanilla
- ⅛ tsp (0.5 mL) baking powder
- ¼ tsp (1.5 mL) lemon or orange zest
- 4 Tbsp (30 g) light brown sugar, packed
- 1 Tbsp (14 g) graham cracker crumbs
- 4 Tbsp (30 g) all-purpose flour

Method

In a greased mug, beat the egg and mix in the cream cheese, ricotta, olive oil, jam and vanilla. Mix well.

Add rest of the ingredients and mix well to form a smooth batter.

Microwave on Power Level 5 (half-power) for 4 to 4½ minutes, or until done.

Sugar Cookie in a Mug

Kind of like a cookie, kind of like a cake, definitely delicious.

Ingredients

    1 Tbsp (15 mL) butter
    1 Tbsp (14 g) sugar
    ¼ tsp (1.5 mL) vanilla extract
    ⅛ tsp (0.5 mL) salt
    1 egg
    3 Tbsp (25 g) all-purpose flour
    Coarse colored sugar (garnish, optional)

Method

Add the butter to a greased mug and microwave for approximately 10 to 20 seconds, until completely melted.

Add the rest of the ingredients and mix well until a smooth batter is formed.

Sprinkle the coarse sugar on top, if desired.

Microwave on Power Level 5 (half-power) for 4 to 4½ minutes, or until done.

Sweet Potato Mug Cake

This easy-to-make mug cakes tastes very much like sweet potato pie! So, save a little leftover, cooked sweet potato and make this amazing dessert.

This recipe makes enough for two, so plan to share, or not, It's up to you.

Ingredients

    1 egg, slightly beaten
    ¼ cup (60 mL) cooked sweet potatoes, mashed
    ¼ cup (60 mL) water
    1 Tbsp (30 mL) whole milk
    ¼ tsp (1.5 mL) vanilla extract
    ¼ cup (45 g) brown sugar, packed
    7 Tbsp (53 g) all-purpose flour
    ⅛ tsp (0.5 mL) salt
    ½ tsp (2.5 mL) ground nutmeg
    ½ tsp (2.5 mL) ground ginger
    3 Tbsp (30 g) chopped walnuts or pecans (optional)

Method

In a small bowl, or 16 oz measuring cup, mix the egg and water together.

Add the sweet potato, milk, vanilla and sugar. Mix well.

Slowly add the flour, spices and salt. Mix well to produce a smooth batter.

Fold in the nuts, if using.

Spoon equal amounts of the batter into two greased mugs.

Microwave each mug separately on Power Level 5 (half-power) for 4 to 4½ minutes, or until done.

Walnut Espresso Mug Cake

This mug cake has a wonderful combination of flavors that compliment each other perfectly.

Ingredients

> 3 Tbsp (25 g) all-purpose flour
> ⅛ tsp (0.5 mL) baking powder
> 1 Tbsp (30 mL) butter, melted
> 4 Tbsp (60 mL) cream
> 1 Tbsp (10 g) espresso coffee powder
> 1 Tbsp (14 g) brown sugar, packed
> 1 Tbsp (10 g) walnuts, chopped

Method

In a greased mug, combine all ingredients (except the walnuts) and mix well to form a smooth batter.

Fold in the walnuts to disperse evenly throughout the batter.

Microwave on Power Level 5 (half-power) for 4 to 4½ minutes, or until done.

Homemade Pumpkin Pie Spice

Bonus Recipe

Making your own pumpkin pie spice is easy.

Ingredients

> 1 teaspoon (5 mL) ground cinnamon
> ¼ teaspoon (1 mL) ground nutmeg
> ¼ teaspoon (1 mL) ground ginger
> ⅛ teaspoon (0.5 mL) ground allspice

Method

Combine all of the ingredients in a small, airtight container. Shake well.

Win A Mug

You can win your choice of either the Vanilla Cake Mug or the Chocolate Cake Mug just by visiting the link below.

http://fun.victoriahousebakery.com/mugcake

About Our Cookbooks

Quality

We are passionate about producing quality cookbooks. You'll never find "cut and pasted" recipes in any of our books.

Consistency

We endeavor to create consistent methods for both ingredients and instructions. In most of our recipes, the ingredients will be listed in the order in which they are used. We also try to make sure that the instructions make sense, are clear and are arranged in a logical order.

Only Quality Ingredients

To ensure that all of our recipes turn out exactly right, we call for only fresh, quality ingredients. You'll never find "ingredients" such as cake mixes, artificial sweeteners, artificial egg replacements, or any pre-packaged items. Ingredients, to us, are items in their natural (or as close to natural as possible), singular form: eggs, milk, cream, flour, salt, sugar, butter, coconut oil, vanilla extract, etc.

About The Author

Vicky Wells and her husband, Geoff, split their time between Ontario, Canada and the island of Eleuthera in the Bahamas. They maintain several websites including GeezerGuides.com which was originally set up for Baby Boomers but has now morphed into the publisher of an eclectic collection of these little booklets.

More information than you could possibly want to know about them is available on their blog http://www.geoffandvickywells.com

Published by Geezer Guides

When you see "Published by Geezer Guides" on any book, you can be confident that you are purchasing a quality product.

Printed in Great Britain
by Amazon